Contents

Before school

Chloe has new clothes for her first day at school.

Munch!

Crunch!

Lenny is excited, but also a bit nervous.

In the cloakroom

Chloe finds out where to hang her coat.

Lenny finds his classroom.

In the classroom

Chloe can read her name on the drawer.

Lenny's teacher is called Mrs Rowe.

9

Everyone is busy

Lenny's class has lots of different coloured felt pens.

11

Playtime

Chloe's friend shows her where the toilets are.

Lenny plays outside with his friends.

Back to the classroom

Chloe is thinking hard about her numbers.

School is fun!

Lunchtime

Chloe is hungry – and ready for her lunch!

Afternoon activities

See how the water swirls and splashes.

Do you like painting?

The day ends

Chloe is choosing a book
from the library.

Do you like singing **action** songs?

Home time

Bye-bye, I'll see you all tomorrow.

Grace   Alex

22

Index

The end

Notes for adults

This series supports the child's knowledge and understanding of their world, in particular their personal, social and emotional development. The following Early Learning Goals are relevant to the series:

- respond to significant experiences, showing a range of feelings where appropriate
- develop an awareness of their own needs, views and feelings and be sensitive to the needs and feelings of others
- develop a respect for their own cultures and beliefs and those of other people
- manage their own personal hygiene
- introduce language that enables them to talk about their experiences in greater depth and detail.

Each book explores a range of different experiences, many of which will be familiar to the child. It is important that the child has the opportunity to relate the content of the book to their own experiences. This will be helped by asking the child open-ended questions, using phrases like: How would you feel? What do you think? What would you do? Time can be made to give the child the chance to talk about their worries or anxieties related to the new experiences.

Talking about school
Starting school is a big step in a child's life and it can be made easier if the child knows their way around the building, has met other new children and knows the name of their teacher. It also helps if they are able to dress/undress independently. The child may find a full day very tiring and needs reassurance that 'home' will be there at the end of the day.

Further activities
These could include setting up a classroom for toys with the child in the role of teacher. A parent can also become a pupil. The child can help make a list of the things that need to be taken to school on different days.